Life Systems

A practical guide to building

a more rewarding life

Neil S. Jorgensen

ISBN: 979-8-9926383-0-1 (paperback)

Library of Congress Control Number: 2025902885

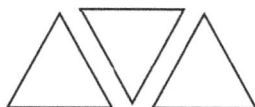

INTRODUCTORY NOTES

How to approach this work

I recommend you, the reader, take a slow, meditative approach to this book. It's most effective when the information seeps in gradually. Repetition is your friend when attempting a significant shift to your life system. This book is intentionally short as it's designed for easy ingestion and to maximize your mind's signal-to-noise ratio. I'm rooting for you.

Have fun

I recommend approaching this system-building method as something fun to experiment with. While the work is powerful, it is very simple. The method is easy to understand. All the work lies within the implementation of the system, so I want to minimize any pretense of this requiring a long learning phase. You should be able to jump right in as soon as you complete this quick read.

This is not self-help

Let's not have this work live in a self-help framework. Even if you're not living the life you want at this moment, a self-help frame is often addictive and dissatisfying in the end and hard to sustain over a lifetime. It's often a state of mind that tells us we are not good enough and have to do more or accomplish more to be lovable. This is a trap we must avoid. You are already lovable. You have accomplished enough. You are here and you are doing your best in a very complicated, unfair, and sometimes cruel world. Opportunity is not distributed equally by any stretch of the imagination. We are all dealt a different hand, with different attributes, constraints, and hardships that we must navigate. Be gentle with yourself as you start this system. Don't be overzealous or you will give up before real change starts to unfold. Slow and steady.

A note on inspiration

This book reflects my journey to organize and distill my own approach to life, but I would be remiss to not mention the foundational impetus and inspiration derived from two simple but powerful books by Daniel Bergevin: Lifestyle Design and Shi. I highly recommend them both if you can track them down. Also, Atomic Habits by James Clear is an important layer to the work and well worth reading. Lastly, 4000 Weeks by Oliver Burkeman is valuable.

This book is not about productivity in the conventional sense, it is about creating forward momentum in your key life categories. It will look different for every single person who takes hold and builds an intentional life system. Lastly, thank you to the inadvertent mentors throughout my life. While never labeled as such, they have taught by example. Pulling threads from inspiring folks is always a good approach. Let's get to it. :)

TABLE OF CONTENTS

1. LIFE IS A SYSTEM

1. Life Is a System

Every one of us utilizes a system to navigate life. It may not be intentionally constructed or understood by us, but it is a system nonetheless.

If we are to thrive, we need to first better understand, then refine and retool our current system. If we are already thriving, it's helpful to know the drivers that support our fortunate circumstances so as to not lose our footing in the future.

There are endless systems we can employ.

Under the surface, every single one of us employs some type of system which encapsulates all of our actions, behavior, and interactions. Each system will vary in its output across a spectrum ranging from hyper productivity to profound lethargy.

A system can move us forward, a system can maintain our current state, and a system can shift us backwards across a wide range of life categories - which would not be pleasant.

Our systems are simply energy distribution in regards to both inputs and outputs. To make a significant foundational change, we must first take inventory of how we deploy energy in our lives.

Once you recognize that you already have a system, the work becomes refinement, reinvention, and retooling.

This book is designed to be simple and leverages repetition to reinforce the key pillars of the work. Simple does not necessarily mean easy. The magic lies in the consistency of application and the spillover effect of this work. I myself don't understand how a system so seemingly simple can become so transformative in our lives, but when properly implemented, that has been my experience.

One can expand. One can implode. One can work within constraint. It may not be easy. It requires a long-term vision and a fortitude of spirit to deploy a new system.

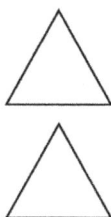

2. INVESTMENTS OF ENERGY

2. Investments of Energy

Life is an investment of energy. Life is in fact an energy distribution system. If we want to thrive in big and little ways, we need to carefully evaluate all our investments of energy in close detail.

Literally everything we do, and every decision we make, is a commitment of time and energy even if very subtle. What we choose to think about, what forms of entertainment we seek, what friends and family we chat with and bounce ideas off, the type of food we choose to eat, the way we treat our bodies, what coworkers, classmates, or strangers we bump into, these are all investments small and large.

It's essential to note that the remit of this book is for you to develop your own system that leverages your strengths and acknowledges your weaknesses. You will design your life system to optimize for what you want within the set of constraints you currently reside in.

Let's take a quick look at why some systems are more effective than others in producing the results we want for our lives.

Every one of us deploys a life system that constitutes a range of recurring action categories. Depending on the balance of action types we are taking on a regular basis, the output of our efforts will provide wildly different results.

Life systems that include a high ratio of actions that propel us forward and help maintain the supportive infrastructure of our lives are typically very effective. When these systems also have the absence of negative or stagnant action categories, then we usually observe the recipe for a rewarding and productive life.

In contrast, if one's life system includes higher ratios of action categories that are not focused on forward motion, especially paired with the types of actions that move us backwards in life, then we typically find the results to be very disappointing in terms of building a fulfilling life. We'll look at the specifics of these mechanics in detail in the coming chapters.

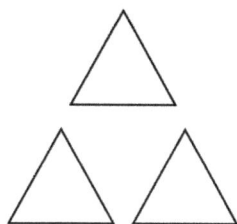

3. SYSTEMS OF LEVERAGE

3. Systems of Leverage

Not all systems are created equal. A system that works for one person will not necessarily produce the same results as it will for someone else. Everyone has a different set of circumstances and a different set of qualities to work with. Depending on our goals, we will need to employ a customized system. Depending on our own strengths and weaknesses, we'll need to tailor our personal system accordingly.

Because we already have an embedded routine and approach to life that can be constituted as a system, we might as well design our own custom system to optimize our lives. We can take it one step at a time for the different categories of our lives or we can find incremental improvements across a wide range of our activities and energy investments.

This approach can and should be applied to any category that suits addressing. Without a system, we can end up in a completely different life than what we want.

Ideally, we can use a system to scratch and crawl our way up from the depths of stagnation into a more vibrant and magical life that feels good, benefits others, and contributes to the world.

Well-constructed systems will slowly create leverage in your life above and beyond just the aggregate sum of your actions. Leverage here can be defined as gaining more output than the required input in terms of results, sometimes at a ratio of many multiples or an order of magnitude in extraordinary cases. Once you develop a strong baseline of daily actions, you will gradually be able to add the subsequent action categories that have the ability to turbo-charge the value proposition of your life.

The first step in developing our own intentional system is to take stock of how we currently employ and deploy energy throughout our lives. To do this, we assign a category label to the different types of actions, and in some cases, non-actions that we take. Initially it's easiest to view this on a daily

3. Systems of Leverage

level. Later in our process, we can zoom out
and look at longer-term action sequences that
we'll utilize to build momentum and multi-
faceted creations in our lives.

First let's start with these action
categorizations. This identification process
is the heart of this work and is meant to
be added onto the contributions that others
have developed around the reinforcements of
habits that propel us forward. It's important
to note that the category names I've chosen
are completely arbitrary. Feel free to make up
your own if there's something that resonates
more closely with your own life.

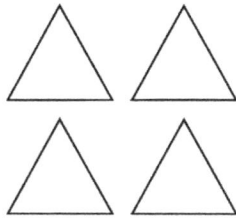

4. CATEGORIZING OUR ACTIONS & NON-ACTIONS

4. Categorizing Our Actions & Non-actions

Here are the action classifications. This is the central tenet of this book as it's a simple way to learn to navigate your life through a new, more organized approach. I'll provide a few examples of each as well. It's very important to understand the qualities of each type of action.

Alpha - an action that builds positive forward momentum and/or helps maintain a positive current state. This is the workhorse of your everyday life. This action class is the rails in which you will be able to gradually move towards a more and more rewarding life. Properly calibrated alphas are absolutely essential to a successful life system.

A few alpha examples: *learning, cleaning, organizing, exercising, practices that quiet your mind, productive work time, caring for a loved one, studying, reading, stretching your comfort zone, proactive financial stewardship, a hike or time spent in nature, journaling, strategic thinking, actions that advance your career trajectory, acts of kindness, implementing good ideas, self-care, and healthy eating.*

Beta - this action class is typically low energy but can also in many cases be considered a treat or reward for accomplishing enough alpha actions within a specific time period. In excess, beta actions will stall you out in life and even move you backwards. You won't be able to or want to eliminate all betas in your life. This would turn you into a type A psychopath. Again, betas when configured properly are leveraged as a reward system for your alpha, sigma, and omega actions. You can enjoy more betas in a given day the more you accomplish. More alphas = more rewards. It's also helpful to understand that this system allows you to enjoy your betas with deeper satisfaction and no guilt. You will become aware of sequencing your rewards properly and will enjoy them fully when you're on track with your system.

A few beta examples: watching television, playing video games, relaxing on the couch,

4. Categorizing Our Actions & Non-actions

doom scrolling on social media (warning: this in excess will become a zeta action), a delicious treat or snack. It's important to note that healthful relaxation (non-screen time) from a productive day is actually an alpha as it sets you up for the next efficient push.

Sigma - helps you grow/expand. Sigma actions extend both your inflows and reach in life.

A few sigma examples: creating visibility for a recent accomplishment, well-executed self-promotion, launching side projects that support your contributions to the world, taking on a new challenge that expands your life, networking, or adding a new skill set. Sigma actions also include intelligently leveraging your assets (social, physical, monetary, etc.) to create additional value.

Omega - helps you and others grow / expand / enrich / connect. Many will benefit from these actions. Often these actions create systems that add recurring value to your life as well as for others.

A few omega examples: *launching a business that employs people with good pay and benefits while also offering the world a valuable product or service, starting a non-profit, sharing information that helps others, and launching scalable ideas. Another example would be an action that helps both your career and the career of others in your network.*

Delta - helping others. Not focused on personal gain. Anonymity. This has great benefits but is not considered a sigma since it's conducted under the radar.

A few delta examples: *anonymous philanthropy, donations, supporting others' needs without asking for anything in return. Many forms of volunteer work fit into this action class.*

Zeta - backwards movement. This category can be defined as your vices, bad habits, and personal demons. The friction and self-sabotage you introduce into your life.

A few zeta examples: dishonesty, cheating, stealing, reckless behavior that leads to injury of yourself or others, activities that cloud your mind, self-doubt, indulging in excessive laziness, and unhealthy food choices. Criminal activity, generally speaking, puts you at risk for massive backwards progress in your life.

It's imperative you scale this category to zero alongside the process of increasing your daily alpha count. Otherwise, your life will be one step forward, two steps back. Zeta actions will counteract your positive progress and at best will create the effect of you merely treading water in life.

A warning on betas

As we scale our alpha count each day, it is really important to understand that betas as rewards need to be closely monitored as many of them add noise to our minds or deplete our overall energy. Be mindful of exactly when you're in a beta action class and be vigilant that it's not in fact deprecating your life force in subtle or obvious ways.

It's also important to understand that betas can and often will, when left unchecked, morph into zetas. If you spend hours scrolling on social media each day, that has very much become a zeta. Our energy is so incredibly valuable and we must be frugal with every one of our investments of time and attention no matter how seemingly small if we are looking to uplevel our lives.

Beware the algorithms

To sharpen the point, we live in a time when the algorithms of capturing your focus, time, and engagement, either in the form of information or entertainment, have become extremely sophisticated. Please be very cautious. You will not be able to resist the machines being built to ensnare your mind if you don't continually resolve that you have a better use of your mental energy and physical time.

Activities that create internal noise and debris in our consciousness will significantly reduce our ability to have true clarity in our lives and achieve a high level of strategic thinking.

Deploying our energy

These action classifications give us an ability to clearly see how we deploy our energy and set the stage for us to onboard a more organized approach to our lives. In doing so, we can produce much more enjoyable results.

The following chapter is how I recommend you start the work, but please customize this to your own life, to where you currently sit, and towards the future state you're aiming for. This is an evergreen exercise that never ends.

It's also important to note that we are not acting in a vacuum. Circumstances beyond our control will surely pop up. We are living in the output, benefits, and constraints of our past system, actions, and choices. There's likely a lot in our lives that we will be navigating, some of which will be friction for forward progress.

Keep it simple

In essence, the system is incredibly simple. First we take an inventory of our daily, weekly, and monthly actions to understand our current balance of action categories. Then we must make small shifts to increase our alpha, sigma, and omega actions, while ensuring our betas are leveraged as a reward system but not an area of overindulgence. Lastly, we need to avoid zetas as an action category at all costs as they can easily erase all our current and future gains. We'll talk more about the specifics in the next section.

Making exceptions

Early in the process, I recommend being as diligent as possible to stay on track for your daily alpha count. There will however be days when you are expending an atypical amount of energy in a new direction and it would be counterproductive, problematic, and potentially impossible to dogmatically stick to completing all your alphas for that day. An example might be a day you need to travel

4. Categorizing Our Actions & Non-actions

for work, a specific family event, or an emergency. Just be very cautious to not seek out excuses for not completing your alphas. The exceptions should generally only be when you are completing less common alphas as a substitute. Thus, you're merely superseding your daily or weekly embedded routine.

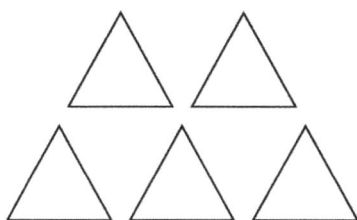

5. ORGANIZING YOUR DAILY SYSTEM

5. Organizing Your Daily System

To jumpstart this work, you'll need to first take an inventory on a daily basis of what types of actions you are taking. Determine and mentally catalog how many of your daily actions are classified as alphas, how many as betas, sigmas, etc.

Calibrating the threshold of your alphas

One note is that every person will have a different threshold for what constitutes a certain action. Depending on your starting point, brushing your teeth, walking your dog, or taking a shower could be considered alphas. Ideally your life already warrants a higher threshold: exercising for 20 minutes or more, preparing and eating a healthy meal, a strong, productive work day, helping a neighbor with a repair, or caring for a loved one.

Your threshold for what defines an alpha will evolve over time. You want to identify an alpha as a bit of a stretch that you need to push yourself to do each day. The proper calibration for an alpha is obtainable on a daily basis with some consistently applied willpower.

The value of this system is it provides just enough extra 'credit' for these alpha actions to inspire you to complete them more diligently than you would without such an intentional process. Before you had a structured approach to your various types of actions, you may not have acted as decisively as you did not truly understand the value, spill-over effect, and cumulative momentum created by such a consciously constructed life system.

Your system will be customized to your life and goals but it's good to start slow. First we need to understand which actions are maintaining our lives, which actions are helping propel us forward, and which actions are likely holding us back and adding negative friction to our lives.

Initial configuration

I recommend a target of *10 alphas per day*. Early on just focus on your alpha/beta actions and avoiding zetas. Later in your process you can ensure you are layering on sigmas, deltas, and omegas into your system.

In the first few months of this work, I highly recommend using a daily checklist that contains your 10 target alphas. If possible, include room for a sigma or omega action item, although these are harder to identify unless you're already thriving and have a sophisticated life system in place. It's ok if these are not a daily occurrence for quite some time. Depending on your goals, they may not constitute a consistent element of your actions even in the future, but keep them in mind as they can truly uplevel your life in unexpected and magical ways. We will explore these action categories in depth in Book 2.

Make a list - copy it if possible or create a matrix where the list covers all 7 days of the week. Your alphas can be organized along the left-hand column with your days of the week flowing out to the right.

Example matrix:

Daily Alphas	MO	TU	WE	TH	FR	SA	SU
morning walk	✓	✓	✓	✓	✓	✓	✓
quiet the mind	✓	✓		✓	✓	✓	✓
productive work day	✓	✓	✓		✓		
act of kindness	✓	✓		✓	✓	✓	✓
healthy meal x 2	✓	✓	✓	✓	✓	✓	✓
push-ups x 100	✓		✓	✓		✓	✓
read for 20 min+	✓	✓	✓		✓		✓
go above & beyond at work	✓	✓		✓	✓		
tidy up home	✓			✓		✓	✓
self-care / daily hygiene routine	✓	✓	✓	✓	✓	✓	✓
bed in time for restful sleep	✓	✓	✓	✓			✓
Total	11	9	7	9	8	7	9

Daily goal - 10 alphas

Remember, these alphas should be a slight stretch. Actions that you need to push yourself to achieve within a day but are feasible and obtainable. You don't need to achieve 10 per day to maintain forward momentum but that should be the target, especially early on when first building this new muscle.

5. Organizing Your Daily System

Refresher on action categories:

Alphas - the workhorse of our life system. These are daily/weekly tasks that build and maintain our personal infrastructure.

Betas - a necessary treat and reward to balance out our proactivity. In excess, they will stunt our lives and lead to stagnation.

Sigmas - actions that expand our lives.

Omegas - benefit multiple people and ourselves. These can be hard to identify.

Deltas - actions that benefit others.

Zetas - actions that create backwards movement and friction. Please avoid.

Internal dialogue

It's really important to know what type of action you are taking as you go through your day and be sure it's in alignment with your new life system. It's helpful to have an ongoing internal dialogue to help you stay on track.

The key to this life system approach lies in balancing our alphas and betas on a granular level. That means knowing in real-time what action class we are engaging in.

As mentioned, alphas and betas balance out each other when properly employed. An effective strategy is to use betas as the reward for completing your daily alphas. As an example, you may crave a specific beta that relaxes you and feels really good. Perhaps it's watching a specific television show or some leisure hobby or activity: you can first sequence a few alphas ahead of this reward. It's much easier to do the hard stuff in advance. You will enjoy the beta much more knowing you're already on track and won't need to muster up the energy after a beta action.

Count your alphas

Count your alphas mentally throughout the day to reinforce the work and give yourself a pat on the back.

If you get to 10 alphas per day, you can always gradually increase the threshold for how you define them and raise the bar, but you'll never need much more than this to provide forward momentum. The point is not to turn into a crazy person always striving for productivity. It should feel calm but productive when you find the right note with this work.

Time of day is very important

Pay close attention to the best time of day to fit in specific alphas in your routine. The first thing you should determine after identifying your alphas is what general time you aim to complete each. Depending on your life's rhythm and obligations, some alphas will be much easier to accomplish at certain times over others.

It's important to keep refining this and be mindful. The idea is not to be a martyr or suffer needlessly through your alphas. The less friction the better. Paying close attention to when you will do each alpha will be crucial to your success with this work.

Stacking alphas

Some alphas can be stacked and this is a very efficient method to knock out at least 10 alphas a day. Pay attention to which you can combine within a sequence to push through a few within a short stretch. It's motivating to know you will reward yourself with a favorite beta activity once you've completed your alphas actions. A beta can also be an opportunity to quickly refuel for the next stack of alphas.

Longer-term action layers

The long-term unlock to adding even more forward momentum to your life will be to layer on sigmas and omegas. This is where magic will start to compound and connection points will start to multiply on their own. Again, we will explore this in detail in Book 2, so for now I recommend keeping your entire focus on balancing your alphas and betas while eliminating your zeta action categories as efficiently as possible.

Above & beyond

If you don't yet have clarity on your life's work, just do an exceptional job with the work and tasks right in front of you. Go above and beyond. This approach will plant the seeds for future opportunities and upliftment. Never take the attitude that you are too good or too smart to do a specific, menial task. In my observations, life will punish you for this state of mind by not offering you opportunities to grow and expand.

The energy we bring to the work, relationships, and interactions of our lives will set the trajectory for our future. We have to bring more to the table than is being asked if we want to uplevel our lives and the lives of those around us. We can't expect to thrive in this world without going above and beyond. With the exception of a very thin sliver at the top of the generational wealth pyramid, life is not a handout. You have to go out and get it and work for it by leveraging a broad spectrum of proactive action categories.

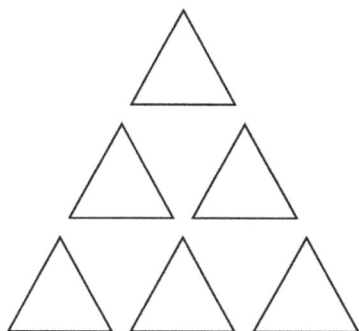

6. DISTILLING YOUR PERSONAL NORTH STAR

6. Distilling Your Personal North Star

I've found that developing a forever north star is a valuable foundation for your life system. It will help keep you on track, it will act as your moral compass, and it will leverage your best qualities. It will help inform your areas of focus and it will contain the essence of what you want from life and what you want to contribute to the world.

I would encourage readers who don't already have one to distill their own north star as part of the work to optimize their life system. It's a layer worth adding that assists us in our long-term navigation of life.

I'll share my personal north star as an example. It's ok and in fact preferable for your north star to be short and concise. This is for you to hold close and it's not meant to be impressive externally. It takes a bit of soul-searching to land on your own but it's a powerful guiding light to your actions. When done properly, your north star will stick with you for the rest of your life.

My own north star

>> *Lead with Warmth*

Start and stop all your relationships, interactions, and touchpoints with warmth.

>> *Connect the Dots*

Help bring people, ideas, and concepts together into new, exciting configurations.

>> *Add More Value*

Add increasing value to the world by leveraging your best self.

Develop your own

Your own north star can be very short. It can be a few bullet points. It should ring true to your timeless essence. It should inspire you and it should push you to be a better person and to give more to humanity, to the planet, and to your loved ones.

Your own north star should feel completely natural. It doesn't need to contain wild aspirations. It's the simple elements of your nature that we want to codify and in doing so we will create a clearly articulated guiding

6. Distilling Your Personal North Star

force for the rest of our lives.

There are already a ton of books on this subject, but I would encourage you to not overthink it. You can refine it over time if it doesn't land with your first attempt, but start somewhere and keep a handwritten copy of it you can revisit often.

It's helpful to consider the throughlines of your life when coming up with your enduring personal north star. Look for the character that has always been with you. Tease out the code that embodies the best version of yourself. Find a way to simply express both who you already are along with who you aspire to be. It's very powerful to have this clarity and a line of sight for your future. This integration of character and action is the foundation for many wonderful things to grow and flourish.

Don't put this off. Draft up your early thoughts and refine them in parallel to taking your action inventory and starting to implement your action-based life system.

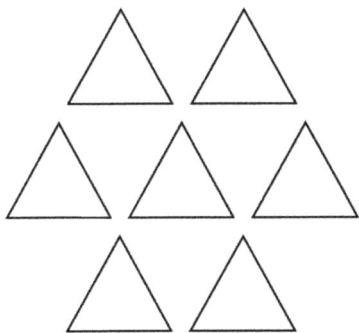

7. THE PATH FORWARD

7. The Path Forward

L et's summarize the approach to ensure the method is clear. Please jump right in, and again, don't overthink it. See if you can embed the work right away. Don't be overzealous but put the early steps in motion starting today.

>> Take an inventory of your planned and/or existing daily alpha actions and create a matrix to track on a weekly basis.

>> Jot down your personal north star to serve as your guiding light for this work and continue to refine it over time. Keep this visible and check back in on it often.

>> Commit to exploring and having fun with this work for the next several months.

>> Stay on track and keep a baseline. Increase the threshold of your alphas gradually, and learn to index towards a quiet and efficient state of mind.

First establish your baseline

What's most important is implementing this work into your life permanently. Over time it will become so integrated that you'll likely drop your physical list because it's become automatic. This doesn't mean you won't continue to need to push yourself and over time gradually raise your thresholds. That being said, done correctly, and with enough consistency, this system will become a part of you and your character. It won't feel like an outside system, it will simply become your own personal ethos, momentum, and trajectory.

In Book 2, we will take a deeper dive into the power of the sigma and omega action categories. These are advanced, so I recommend a solid 6 months of focus on refining your alpha baseline before exploring this next layer.

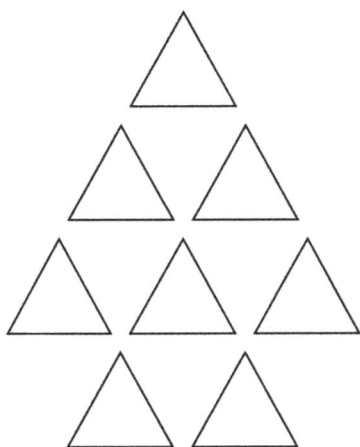

8. ONGOING REFINEMENTS

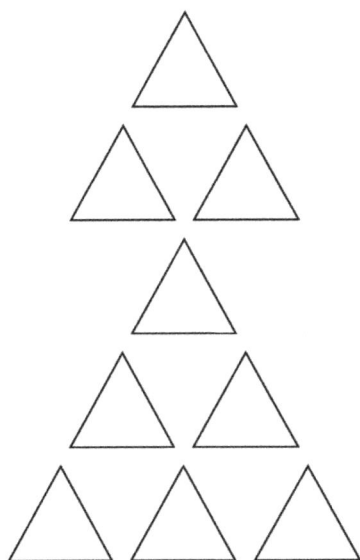

9. THE PROFOUND VALUE OF A QUIET MIND

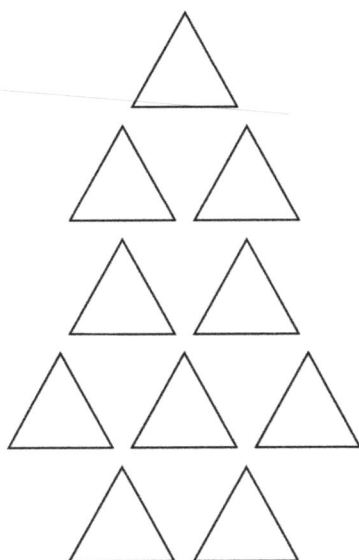

10. PATIENCE & PERSEVERANCE

8. Ongoing Refinements

The start of this work is the very beginning of a lifelong process of refinement to your system. Circumstances will change, life will throw new challenges at you, and it's your system that will need to be agile. There will be days when there's just not enough time and energy to check through your alphas. That's ok. What's most important is that you get back on track as quickly as possible.

Momentum with this work is contagious. It will spill over into new areas of your life and it will build upon itself in ways you will not be able to predict.

When embedding new daily actions, it's important to start small. As I've mentioned several times, I discourage an overzealous approach as it's not sustainable. It's been said that new recurring actions in our lives should be short and simple when first being integrated into your schedule and routines. I have found this to be very true. Start small and never stop iterating. Stay committed as you make your adjustments and you will truly thrive.

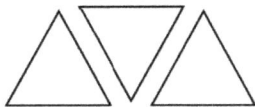

ABOUT THE AUTHOR

About the Author

The author grew up in the redwoods of a small town nestled in the mountains of California. He now calls the high desert of New Mexico home. In between, he spent years in San Francisco, New York, and Los Angeles.

He's inhabited his truck, a yurt, a mid-century modernist residence, city lofts, and an adobe house. He holds a strong love for architecture and natural landscapes.

His eclectic career includes a stint in investment banking, Michelin-starred cooking experience, restaurant ownership, and big tech with lots of tangential jobs along the way. Many twists and turns. Many ups and downs. Many distinct chapters. He grew tired of being bounced around by life and built a system to intentionally navigate this world - the foundation of this book series.

10. Patience & Perseverance

T his work takes time. It takes consistent practice for it to become deeply embedded in your life and habits. You are reworking your entire ecosystem of energy. It is a lifelong pursuit. As you do the work, you will be drawn to constantly make small tweaks that optimize your time and your results.

Start with a daily checklist to ensure you are moving towards more alphas and mitigating excess betas in your routine. Long-term we will strive to find as many sigmas and omegas as possible, but your alphas alone will give you forward momentum that you can build on with time. If you do have zetas in your life, work hard to eliminate them.

Go slow. Gradual, incremental change is powerful. Be patient with yourself and you will begin to see signs of your new life sprouting up in all sorts of ways both obvious and subtle.

Once again, I'm rooting for you.

9798992638301